At The Changing of the Year

A play

MALCOLM YOUNG

SAMUEL FRENCH

LONDON
NEW YORK TORONTO SYDNEY HOLLYWOOD

CHARACTERS

Janet
Ian, her husband
Dave
Julia, his wife
Lavinia
Edward
A Man at the Door (voice only)

The action takes place in the sitting-room of an early Victorian house in the depths of the country, late evening

Time—last New Year's Eve

AT THE CHANGING OF THE YEAR

The drawing-room of an old country house. Last New Year's Eve

A wide archway at the back leads off to the front door and to the stairs and the rest of the house

When the CURTAIN *rises the room is in semi-darkness. Only a few candles light the heavy Victorian furniture. (See special note in Lighting Plot, p. 17)*

Janet, an elegant woman, enters from the hall with two lighted branch candelabra, which she places in suitable positions, then checks the room in obvious anticipation of guests. Ian, her husband, comes downstairs and into the room, calling as he does so

Ian Darling! Ah, there you are. Oh I say, how romantic.

Janet I found another box of candles.

Ian Well done. Makes the old place look a lot better.

Janet Can't see the dust, you mean.

Ian Well that too.

Janet Give me a hand with this table, will you?

Ian Janet, it's been everywhere. Where do you want it now?

Janet Over there.

Ian But that's where it was to start with.

Janet I know. Just proves my first ideas are always best. Come on.

Ian All right. There. Happy now?

They move the table

Janet I *think* so. Ian darling, this settee's really not right here, you know.

Ian It stays. Tomorrow if you like, but tonight it stays. Anyway, I nearly forgot why I came down. Where's my bow tie? I can't find a damned thing upstairs in all the gloom.

Janet Heavens, Ian, I don't know where it is. You packed all *your* things.

Ian I thought I left my chest of drawers to you.

Janet So you did. Sorry. Well I think all the odds and ends from there went into the red trunk.

Ian Is that unpacked yet?

Janet Not completely. I made a start. As a matter of fact that's what I was doing when the lights went. Darling, are you quite sure you've checked everything?

Ian Well I think so but I wouldn't swear to it. I'll get Dave to have a look when they arrive.

Janet *If* they arrive. It's still snowing hard.

Ian It'll be a white New Year.

Janet I'm just grateful it waited until we were moved in. How does the room look?

Ian Don't fuss darling. It's only Dave and Julia.

Janet I know, but I want it to look nice, our first guests and all that.

Ian Considering that it's less than forty-eight hours since we moved in and that we've suddenly been plunged into total darkness, I think you've performed miracles, my love. (*He kisses her lightly*) And now to the depths of the red trunk.

Janet If it's not there it must be in that big Weetabix box.

Ian Logical! And where's that?

Janet All right, I'll find it. You see if you can open that tin of biscuits, will you?

Ian It's a deal.

Janet exits upstairs

After a moment there is a knocking at the front door

Ian (*moving towards the door*) Darling, they're here.

Ian exits to the hall

Ian (*off*) Oh, Good evening.

Man (*off*) Evenin', gov'nor. Special deliv'ry.

Ian (*off*) What?

Man (*off*)) Package for the mistress. Sorry to be so late sir. Snow's getting quite thick on the other side of the hill. Anyway, 'Appy New Year to you, gov'nor.

Ian (*off*) Oh, yes, thank you. Er, will you come inside and have a drink?

Man (*off*) Thanks all the same, gov'nor, but I want to be 'ome in time to see the New Year in with the missus. They say there's a sight more snow to come yet. Good night then, sir.

Ian (*off*) Good night.

The door closes and Ian enters with a small box. He discovers an envelope tucked into the wrapping, reads the name and hurries back to the door

Ian I say . . .

The door closes again and Ian returns, as Janet comes down the stairs with Ian's tie

Janet Where are they? Who was that?
Ian What a peculiar thing.
Janet What?
Ian It was a parcel.
Janet Being delivered at this time of night? You must be joking.
Ian I know, and in this weather too. But look. A funny old chap he was, all muffled up. He just thrust this into my hands; "for the mistress," he said.
Janet For me, you mean?
Ian Well no, that's just the point. By the time I'd read the name on the envelope he'd gone.
Janet Let me see. Oh here's your tie.
Ian Thanks.
Janet "Miss Lavinia Harcourt." Well, who's that?
Ian I don't know. Perhaps the old chap came to the wrong house.
Janet With our nearest neighbour a mile and a half away? I should think that most unlikely.
Ian Well I can't think of a better explanation, can you?

Ian moves to the mirror and begins to tie his bow

Janet No, not really. The envelope isn't sealed. Shall I just peep and see if there's an address inside?
Ian You know what curiosity did, don't you? Is this tie straight? (*At the mirror he turns, and is surprised that Janet is on the other side of the room*) Good Lord! I could have sworn that you were standing right behind me. I honestly could have sworn that I saw your reflection right behind me. What a strange thing. Candles are all very fine and romantic but I can't see a damned thing in this mirror.
Janet It's fine. Shall I open it then?
Ian Darling, it's quite obvious you won't survive the night unless you do.

Janet (*opening the envelope and reading*) "Lavinia. Hope to be with you at Court Barton in time for midnight. My love, Edward."

Ian At Court Barton? Here? But there must be some mistake. Let me see. (*He takes the note and reads*) "Hope to be with you by midnight."

Janet Ian, I don't like it.

Ian What do you mean?

Janet I can't explain. It's just a feeling I have—strange, unnatural. When I read that note I went cold all over. I felt as though I were intruding—intruding into a whole world belonging to someone else.

Ian You are a hopeless romantic, aren't you?

Janet Don't laugh darling. Oh I suppose I am being silly. Maybe it's what I said last night about having bought the house with all the furniture. It still feels like someone else's house. And now this letter. I just don't like it.

Ian Let's have a drink. (*He moves to the drinks table and pours two drinks*)

Janet again reads the note and looks at the parcel

You know, there's probably a very simple explanation for it. Lord, look at the time. (*He goes to the window*) It's still snowing like hell out there. I just hope Dave and Julia don't get stuck somewhere.

Janet What shall we do?

Ian What, if they don't turn up?

Janet No, about the parcel.

Ian Well I don't see that there's much we can do. Not tonight anyway, so forget about it. Here's your drink. Cheers! (*He drinks and sits*)

Janet (*sitting*) It seems such a shame. I wonder if he doesn't know that she's moved. Ian! He's probably on his way here right now.

Ian Darling, the old lady who lived here had been living alone for donkey's years, and anyway, *her* name wasn't Lavinia.

Janet What *was* her name?

Ian I can't remember, but it wasn't Lavinia. I'd have remembered that.

Janet So somewhere poor Lavinia could be sitting and thinking that her Edward has forgotten all about her.

Ian Oh come on darling, you've been reading too many novels.

They both laugh

Here's to Lavinia and her dear Edward.

They drink

Listen!

Janet (*jumping nervously*) What?

Ian Darling don't be so jumpy. I thought I heard a car, that was all.

Janet I'm sorry. I just feel all on edge.

Ian Jan, I've told you, there's probably a very simple explanation.

Janet Like what?

Ian (*rising and crossing to the window*) Well, I don't know.

Janet I wish we were on the telephone.

Ian Why?

Janet I was just thinking if Dave and Julia can't get through they'd surely ring, and then I remembered.

Ian (*returning and sitting*) Mm. Does make one feel a bit cut off. But that's what we wanted wasn't it? One of the main reasons we've moved to the country. Get away from it all. Wasn't that the idea?

Janet I know but it'll take some getting used to. Like the quiet. Listen. Not a sound.

They listen for a moment. Suddenly Ian rises

Ian There it is again. (*Moving to the window*) It *is* a car. It must be them. Oh Lord, it sounds as though they're stuck down the drive.

Janet (*rising*) Oh no.

Ian (*moving to the hall*) I'll go and have a look with the torch.

Janet Put a coat on.

Ian All right.

Ian exits to the front door

Janet picks up the parcel. She opens the envelope and reads again

Janet "Lavinia. Hope to be with you at Court Barton in time for midnight. My love, Edward." (*She returns the card to the envelope and replaces the parcel on the table*)

The sound of a musical box playing "Auld Lang Syne" is heard faintly on the air, from nowhere and everywhere. Janet spins round to trace the source of the sound. It stops. She presses her hand to her head and sits. The music starts again and she jumps up. Now it is louder and more insistent. Janet finds herself unable to move

A pale, almost transparent, crinolined figure enters the room, crosses Janet and takes the parcel. The woman pauses and looks round the room as though sensing a presence; but seeing no-one she moves on and out

The music stops suddenly. Janet falls in a faint as the front door opens

Dave (*off*) She suddenly slid into the ditch and stuck there.

Julia (*off*) And now it looks as though you're going to be stuck with us for the night.

Ian (*off*) The pleasure's ours if you don't mind the primitive. Sorry about the lighting situation. Everything went out at seven o'clock. I think it must be a cable down somewhere with the snow.

Ian enters the room, followed by Dave and Julia

Darling, they're here. Jan? Darling, where are you? (*He sees Janet*) Oh my God!

Dave What is it?

Julia What's the matter?

Ian Janet. Darling. Whatever's happened?

Janet (*coming around and beginning to sob*) Oh darling, darling . . .

Ian Dave, pour some brandy will you?

Dave goes and pours a brandy

Now take it easy, darling. Come and sit down and tell me what happened.

Janet I—I must have fainted. Oh Ian it was horrible.

Ian What was?

Dave Brandy.

Ian Thanks Dave. Here, drink this.

Janet No, I don't want it.

Ian Drink it.

Janet drinks

Now tell me quietly.

Janet Dave, Julia, I'm so sorry. What a welcome for you.
Julia Hello, darling. No, don't get up. Just you take it easily.
Ian It's not like you darling. I've never known you to faint before.
Janet I feel better now, truly.
Ian It's all been a bit much I expect, moving house coming bang
  on top of Christmas.
Dave I say, I should think you could well have done without us.
Ian Good Lord no. Why do you think we asked you? You and
  Julia are like family. Come on, Julia, let me take your coat.
Julia It's O.K. (*Moving to the hall*) I'll hang it out here, shall I?
Ian Fine thanks. (*Going to pour drinks*) Now, come and sit down
  and have a drink and thaw out.

Julia stands transfixed in the hall entrance

Dave What's the matter Julia?
Julia What? Oh, sorry. I was just thinking—what an interesting
  room. It seems familiar somehow. You know how sometimes
  you think you've been somewhere before when you know per-
  fectly well that you haven't? (*Coming into the room*) Jan
  darling, are you sure you're all right?
Janet Yes, honestly thanks. I really don't know what came over
  me.
Ian (*going*) What's your poison, Julia? The usual?
Julia Please, darling. Not too much tonic.
Ian Scotch, Dave?
Dave Thanks. Do you know, 1 honestly thought we weren't going
  to make it. The snow's much thicker over on the other side of
  the hill.
Ian That's what our midnight postman said.
Julia Your what?
Ian Rather strange really. There was a knock on the door just a
  little while before you arrived. As a matter of fact we thought it
  was you. Instead of which it was a peculiar old chap all muffled
  up like something out of the last century who said . . .
Janet (*standing suddenly*) Why do you say that?
Ian Say what?
Janet About "like something out of the last"—you know.
Ian Darling, what is it? It was just an expression.
Julia Look Jan, why don't you go and lie down for a while?
  I mean, don't mind us.

Janet But honestly, I'm quite all right now.

Ian I think Julia's right, darling. Just for half an hour. You can get up again in time for midnight.

Dave You do look pretty ghastly you know, Jan.

Janet But really . . .

Ian No arguments. Come on, I'll take you up.

Julia We'll see you later, darling.

Janet All right.

Ian Help yourselves to another drink, Dave. Shan't be a couple of minutes.

Dave Okay. Thanks.

Ian and Janet exit up the stairs

Dave takes Julia's glass and moves to the drinks table

Dave Poor old Jan.

Julia Something funny going on.

Dave What do you mean?

Julia It's not like Jan.

Dave Perhaps she's pregnant.

Julia She's not.

Dave How do you know she's not?

Julia I don't know that she's not but I'd know if she was.

Dave Feminine logic!

Julia Dave, did you notice what she said when she came round?

Dave What?

Julia She said, "It was horrible". It was as though she'd had some terrible fright and for some reason she wouldn't say anything. Perhaps she'll tell Ian now.

Dave We shouldn't have come. It's what Ian said, it's all been too much for her.

Julia But that's not like Janet. She's always taken everything in her stride. No, there's something strange about this place. I noticed it the minute we walked in through that front door.

Dave Oh my God, did you pack your crystal ball?

Julia Don't joke about it, Dave, you know I can tell about these things.

Dave And what can you tell?

Julia I sense something. There's a kind of presence in this house.

Dave Now look, Julia, stop before you start, will you? I mean it. Otherwise you'll get all worked up and we shan't sleep a wink tonight. Hell, my eyes are burning. It's a terrific strain driving through snow like that at night.

Ian enters

Ian Sorry about all that.

Julia Is she all right?

Ian Well I don't honestly know. She's behaving most strangely. I'm really rather worried.

Dave Do you think you ought to call a doctor?

Ian Well actually I think I'd quite like to, just to be on the safe side, but with no phone and a mile and a half to the village it seems rather out of the question.

Julia Shall I go up and sit with her?

Ian Well I did say I'd go straight back up. She seems awfully on edge.

Julia You sit down. I'll go up. Where is it?

Ian Thanks Julia. It's the second on the left at the top of the stairs. I left the door open.

Julia goes into the hall. The sound of the musical box is heard. Julia stops, looking up the stairs

Julia Oh, she's coming down. Janet? (*Her expression changes*) Janet? Dave, Ian, come and look quickly.

As Dave and Ian rush forward, the music suddenly stops

Dave What is it?

Ian What's the matter? What are you staring at?

Julia Didn't you see anything? I thought I saw . . .

Ian rushes off up the stairs calling "Janet"

Dave Whatever was all that about?

Julia I was right, Dave. I saw something—someone.

Dave Oh for God's sake don't start that again, letting your imagination run away with you like that. It's not fair, putting the wind up everyone. Surely you can see how worried Ian is.

Julia I was not imagining things; and please do not shout at me. Anyway . . .

Dave All right, all right! Here's Ian coming down.

Ian enters

Julia Is she all right?

Ian She's asleep. What did you see, Julia?

Julia I'm sorry, Ian, a mistake. I thought I saw Janet coming down. It must have been a trick of the light or something.

Dave Can I help us all to another drink? We all seem to be getting rather edgy. (*He goes to pour drinks*)

Ian Yes, of course, thanks, Dave. Oh honestly, you two, I'm really sorry about all this. What a way to welcome you to our new house.

Dave Stop apologizing. It's us. Remember? Drink this.

Ian Thanks.

Dave Julia? Freshen it?

Julia What? No, I'm all right thanks.

Ian Well in spite of everything it really is good to see you both.

Dave Good health.

They all sit

Julia It *would* have been more sensible for you to have come to us.

Ian You know Jan couldn't wait to have you down. Mind you, I've been dying myself for you to see this place. It really was something of a bargain.

Dave We'll have to take your word for it until morning.

Julia It's too much.

Dave What is?

Julia Us staying. There was a pub back in the village. We should see if they can put us up there.

Ian Julia, what nonsense. I've already told you . . .

Julia But really . . .

Ian I won't hear of it. And neither will Jan.

Julia But, Dave, I don't think we should.

Dave I told you, Julia, stop it!

Ian (*rising*) Listen, Jan was hiding something from me. She's the world's worst liar. And now I think *you're* trying to hide something from me. What did you think you saw just now, Julia?

Dave Oh forget it, Ian. It's the surroundings—I mean, well what with the snow and the wind howling outside like this, and this dreadful gloom—ha! Sorry, no offence meant, but it's enough

to get anyone's imagination working overtime, leave alone
Julia's. You know what Julia's like.
Ian I'd still like to know what you thought you saw Julia. Julia?
Julia Dave's probably right, Ian. It must have been my imagina-
tion.
Ian Well I don't think *I'm* imagining things. There's been some-
thing strange, just little things mainly, but an atmosphere I
can't quite describe, ever since the old chap brought that
parcel.
Dave What parcel?
Ian Oh, that's what I started to tell you . . . Where is it?
Julia What?
Ian There was a . . . Have either of you moved a parcel from
that table?
Julia No.
Dave Of course not.
Ian Then where is it?
Julia (*rising*) Listen!

*The sound of the musical box is heard again. They freeze, listening.
It breaks off as Janet is heard to scream*

Ian rushes off up the stairs

Julia Take me away from here, Dave.
Dave (*rising*) But . . .
Julia Please, Dave, don't let's even discuss it. I can't stay here
I'm frightened.
Dave You seem to have forgotten that the car's in a ditch at the
bottom of the drive.
Julia Then we'll walk to the village. Please, Dave, I can't stand
it. I knew the moment we came in and now I'm sure. I have
this feeling, I'm convinced if we stay here something terrible
will happen.
Dave Now you *are* being ridiculous.
Julia I'm not staying in this house another minute. If you won't
come with me I shall go alone.
Dave Stop it, for Heaven's sake. You're getting hysterical.
(*Going to the window*) Just look at that blizzard blowing, will
you? It's even worse than when we arrived.

Ian enters with the musical box

Ian She's still asleep.
Dave She screamed in her sleep? Bad dream, I expect.
Ian This was on the bedside table.
Julia What is it?

Ian opens the musical box and it plays

Dave There you are. I said there was quite a rational explanation.
Ian It's not quite as simple as that, Dave. (*He shuts the box*) This was the parcel the old chap brought, the one I was telling you about. We didn't open it, we just read the card, this card. And then it was left on that table. Neither Janet nor I could have taken it upstairs.
Dave Surely Janet could have taken it up when you came down the drive to meet us?
Ian Possibly, but I'd be willing to swear that it wasn't upstairs when I took Jan up. I would have been bound to see it.
Dave But that *was* what we all heard just now.
Julia But then it seemed to be here. The sound seemed to be in this room.
Ian I just cannot understand how it could have got upstairs. Unless . . .
Julia Unless what?
Ian Oh nothing; forget it. (*He puts the box on the table*)
Julia I'm sorry, Ian, I can't just forget it. You're thinking the same thing that I am and it's no use going on pretending. Even if Dave won't listen to me, please will you? Please can we use your car? Go and get Jan and let's try to get to the village, find the pub, anything. You could find a doctor to see her. You said you wanted to.
Dave I'm sorry Ian, Julia's hysterical. She's always . . .
Ian No, I think she may be right. There is something very odd. Whatever kind of explanation you might find for that musical box being upstairs, however rational it might be, I don't think I'd quite believe it.
Dave But that's imagination taking over.
Julia You're outvoted. Ian agrees we should go.
Ian Well, I didn't exactly say that, Julia.
Dave Of course you didn't. It's ridiculous, at this time of night to go careering off into the filthiest possible weather just because you imagine . . .

Julia Dave, this is not just imagination. What's got to happen before you'll believe me?

Janet appears in the hall entrance

Janet What are you all arguing about?
Ian Darling, how do you feel now?
Janet I'm all right. I couldn't sleep.
Dave Come and sit down, Jan.

Janet sits

Ian You were sound asleep when I came up just now.
Janet I didn't hear you.
Julia We heard you cry out in your sleep. We thought you must have been having a bad dream.
Janet This whole evening seems a bit like a bad dream.
Ian How?
Janet You know the old thing about seeing around corners? You know how sometimes you think you know the very next thing that's going to happen? It's what you said when you came in, Julia.
Julia What did I say?
Janet I don't remember exactly but it was something about this place seeming familiar, about thinking you'd been here before. That's precisely the feeling I've had all evening.
Dave But there's a perfectly well-known explanation for that sort of thing. It's something to do with one half of the brain reacting a fraction of a second before the other.
Julia Oh do shut up, Dave, and let Jan finish what she was saying.
Janet Something happened when Ian came out to meet you. I don't know what it was, I can't remember. But I know that it was something strange and unnatural. And then just now, when I was upstairs I had the same feeling and I couldn't open my eyes. Not because I was afraid or anything like that, I just couldn't. But it was as though there was a presence in the room. What time is it?
Dave Almost midnight.
Janet Almost midnight. The last minutes of the old year ticking slowly away. All over the world people must be thinking the same thoughts. Thinking over the past year, the good, the bad

things that have happened. And at the same time they are thinking about the year to come, wondering what lies in store for them. If there does exist a dimension of Time which as yet we don't understand, I believe that it is right now, with so many thoughts feeling into the past —and into the future, that the secrets of that unknown dimension must be most vulnerable.

Julia Please, I'm frightened. Don't let's stay here any longer. Something terrible is going to happen at midnight, I feel it, I know it.

Janet I feel it too. Ian, go and start the car. Let's leave this place.

Ian But . . .

Janet Please, don't let's argue. I've felt something about this house ever since we came here, and now Julia feels it too I'm convinced.

Dave There you are, I told you you'd get everyone worked up.

Janet It's almost midnight. Hurry, Ian.

Dave But this is ridiculous.

Ian Oh there's no point in arguing with them. Let's try, though I doubt if we'll get further than the end of the drive.

Ian exits through the front door

Dave Of all the harebrained . . . Hang on, Ian, I'll give you a hand.

Dave exits through the front door

Janet We aren't just being hysterical over nothing, are we?

Julia No, I'm sure we're not.

Janet I've never felt more certain over anything in my whole life. I just seem to know that if we don't leave this place before midnight we never shall. Come on, Julia.

Julia Don't you want a coat?

Janet There's no time. We must hurry.

Julia and Janet exit through the front door

The car is heard starting, voices, doors slamming. The car leaves as the clock begins to strike midnight. On the fourth stroke there is a screech of brakes and a tremendous crash. The clock continues, and on the eleventh stroke a knocking is heard at the door

The woman in the crinoline comes down the stairs. She is on

*longer pale and transparent, but bright and very real. She crosses
the hall and opens the front door*

Lavinia (*off*) Edward. You're here at last. Come in.

Edward, looking rather shaken, enters with Lavinia

Whatever's the matter, Edward? You look as though you've
seen a ghost.

Edward I think I have.

Lavinia What?

Edward As I came into the drive a strange shadow came hurtling
towards me and it seemed to swerve to avoid me. It appeared to
burst into flames and in the flames I seemed to see people
struggling to be free. It only lasted a few seconds and then it
was gone.

Lavinia How horrible, dearest. Let me pour you a drink. (*She
pours a drink*)

Edward I don't think it was just my imagination.

Lavinia (*handing Edward his drink*) Here you are. You're here
now, let's not think about it. I'm so pleased that you got here
by midnight. Oh, thank you for my musical box. It was a
lovely thought.

Edward I'm so glad you like it.

Lavinia (*seeing the musical box on the table*) What a strange
thing.

Edward What?

Lavinia I could have sworn that I took it upstairs.

Edward Well, how about a toast?

Lavinia Oh yes.

Edward What else? Here's to the New Year.

Edward
Lavinia } To eighteen seventy-nine.* (*Speaking together*)

The musical box plays, as—

the CURTAIN *falls*

* The year one hundred previous to that in which the play is produced
should be inserted here.

FURNITURE AND PROPERTY LIST

On stage: Settee
2 armchairs
2 upright chairs
Drinks table. *On it:* decanters of whisky, brandy, gin, sherry, tonic water, opener, assorted glasses, tin of biscuits
Sideboard. *On it:* dressing, candles (lit) in candle-sticks
Whatnot. *On it:* dressing, candle (lit) in stick
Grandfather clock
Occasional table
Other furniture as desired
Carpet
Heavy window curtains, drawn throughout

Off stage: 2 lighted candelabra **(Janet)**
Front door knocker (for use of **Cast**)
Wrapped musical box **(Man at Door)**
IAN's bow tie **(Janet)**

LIGHTING PLOT

Special note: The play was originally produced without any electric lighting, and where fire regulations permit it is ideal that the only lighting should be from candles. Should it be necessary to use covering spots, these should be kept as low as possible. The only cue is **Janet's** first entrance, when some increase of light should be brought in to cover the places where she puts the candelabra

EFFECTS PLOT

Cue 1   **Janet** replaces musical box on table   (Page 5)
*Sound of musical box playing "Auld Lang Syne",
seemingly all around the room: stop, then re-start
louder: stop suddenly as* **Woman** *exits*

Cue 2   **Julia** goes into hall   (Page 9)
Sound of musical box off: stop suddenly as **Dave**
and **Ian** *rush forward*

Cue 3   **Julia:** "Listen!"   (Page 11)
Sound of musical box off: stop as **Janet** *screams*

Cue 4   **Ian** opens musical box   (Page 12)
Musical box plays: stop when he shuts lid

Cue 5   After **Janet** and **Julia** leave   (Page 14)
*Sounds of car starting, doors slamming, car
leaving. Clock strikes midnight. On fourth stroke
—a screech of brakes and tremendous crash*

All these sound effects are available on record or cassette from
Samuel French Ltd.

MADE AND PRINTED IN GREAT BRITAIN BY
LATIMER TREND & COMPANY LTD PLYMOUTH
MADE IN ENGLAND